ALBION *and* CROSSLEY

Buses in camera

ALBION *and* CROSSLEY

Buses in camera

Stewart J. Brown MCIT

LONDON

IAN ALLAN LTD

BODY BY
CHAS. H. ROE 1923 LTD.
CROSSGATES
LEEDS
PHONE: X GATES 93 GRAMS: VEHICLES
LEEDS
EMERGENCY EXIT
104
Crossley
UA-5854
P177

Contents

Previous page, left: A Venturer SP81 from the first batch of Albion double-deckers delivered to Glasgow Corporation. New in 1935 it had 52-seat Cowieson bodywork and a Gardner 6LW engine. *R. L. Grieves collection*

Previous page, right: The impressive front end of the Crossley Condor is clearly illustrated in this view of one of seven delivered to Leeds Corporation in 1930. This one had a 48-seat Roe body. *Charles H. Roe*

Front cover
Left: In 1937-38 Albion supplied 15 three-axle Valkyries to Young's Bus Service of Paisley. This vehicle was ultimately operated by Highland Omnibuses of Inverness, and survived until 1956. The bodywork was by Cowieson of Glasgow.
G. Morant

Right: Typifying Crossley's postwar double-deck production is this 1947 DD42 in the Sunderland Corporation fleet. It has Crossley bodywork. *G. Morant*

First published 1982

ISBN 0 7110 1191 5

Published by Ian Allan Ltd, Shepperton, Surrey; and printed by Ian Allan Printing Ltd at their works at Coombelands in Runnymede, England

Introduction

For those who find Albion and Crossley strange bedfellows let me start with an explanation. They are here not so much for what they have in common — both are 'vanished makes' — but for what divides them. Between them they cover the country quite effectively. Crossleys sold best in England; Albions in Scotland and Wales. They cover different sections of the industry. Crossley sold to municipalities; Albion to company operators; both to independents. Their product ranges over the years differed. Crossley built trolleybuses; Albion built underfloor-engined chassis. At their postwar peak new Crossleys outnumbered new Albions — but Albion started building buses before Crossley and were still building them, albeit under Leyland ownership, after the last Crossleys had disappeared from public service.

So they are here for the contrast they offer. Coincidentally both can be considered part of the heritage of Britain's biggest remaining bus builder, Leyland Bus. Albion was purchased directly by Leyland Motors in 1951 and continued to build for markets where Leyland was poorly represented. Crossley was taken over by AEC which was subsequently merged with Leyland, though by that time Crossley's products had long been out of production and the factory closed.

In a volume this size I have not tried to detail the history of each company. I have rather tried to give some idea of the products they built; how these developed through the years; and to whom they were sold. I hope that the illustrations which follow have achieved this.

Acknowledgements

Thanks are due to everyone who contributed photographs; their work is credited as appropriate. In addition Roy Marshall provided many photographs from his collection which are credited to their original sources (where known) and Geoff Lumb provided copies of photographs from the Roberts and Strachans collections, aided and abetted by Bob Smith. Ian Maclean provided invaluable comments on early Albion models — but any erroneous conclusions drawn or opinions expressed are mine, not his. Others who helped but who do not get due credit elsewhere include Gavin Booth, Michael Corcoran, Graham Ewing, Robert Grieves, Reg Ludgate and Colin Martin. The PSV Circle kindly gave permission to quote from its records.

Stewart J. Brown
Withnell Fold, 1982

Below: Leeds City Tramways bought four of Crossley's new Eagle chassis in 1929 and had them fitted with 32-seat Roe bodywork. *Charles H. Roe*

Above: An Albion Venturer CX19 for Hutchison of Overtown fitted with the only double-deck body to be built by Stewart of Wishaw. The body framing was supplied by Cowieson of Glasgow, and the bus had a general appearance not dissimilar to contemporary Glasgow Corporation vehicles. It was new in 1939. *R. L. Grieves collection*

Below: Some of the New South Wales Department of Road Transport & Tramways' Albion Venturers seen crossing the Sydney Harbour Bridge in the late 1940s. The traffic contains an interesting mixture of British and American cars. *R. L. Grieves collection*

Albion

Sure as the Sunrise

The Albion Motor Car Company Ltd was founded in December 1899 by T. Blackwood Murray and Norman Fulton. Based in Scotstoun, a few miles to the west of Glasgow's city centre, Albion initially produced 8hp dog carts with horizontally-opposed two-cylinder engines. Some of these early vehicles saw use as hotel buses, and by 1905 they were operating in Sutherland as postbuses with bodywork designed to carry mail and passengers.

The 16hp model which was introduced in 1903 was frequently used as a charabanc. However, Albion's involvement in cars was comparatively short-lived. In 1913 the company elected to concentrate on commercial vehicles — its larger car chassis were already frequently used as such.

The 3ton truck chassis was built in large quantities for the War Office during World War 1. This had a 32hp four-cylinder engine and a three-speed gearbox. It was chain driven and, with large chain sprockets to increase speed, saw service as a charabanc.

By the mid-1920s it was becoming increasingly clear that there was a large market for purpose-built bus chassis. This was the era of expansion in bus operation. Prior to the passing of the 1930 Road Traffic Act bus operators enjoyed a high degree of freedom. On town services buses were more flexible than tramcars on country routes they were cheaper and more convenient than trains.

So in 1925 Albion became one of the first manufacturers to introduce a proper low-frame bus chassis. The development of Albion's model range is catalogued in the pages which follow. An image of reliability was — justifiably — promoted. The motto 'Sure as the Sunrise' was coined to further this image and radiator badges incorporated a burst of sun rays, a feature which survived in various forms for almost 50 years.

Albions were, generally, conservative. Although diesel engines were made available from 1933, Albion was less active in their promotion than most other manufacturers. Also, when most manufacturers produced entirely new models after World War 2, Albion was content to continue offering what were largely unchanged prewar CX-series chassis.

Control of Albion Motors Ltd (the title of the company since 1931) passed to Leyland Motors in July 1951 and Albion's bus range was immediately pruned. The last full-size heavy-duty buses for the British market entered service in 1952, appropriately in Albion's native city: a batch of Venturers for Glasgow Corporation.

Under Leyland ownership Albion developed the Victor for home and overseas markets, and then moved up to heavier truck-based bus chassis aimed at the needs of developing countries. A few products did appear with British operators in mind, but all were heavily influenced by Leyland. Double-deck production even reappeared briefly with the Lowlander, designed to meet the needs of the Scottish Bus Group.

In 1971 the use of the Albion name was dropped by Leyland, although both Albion and Leyland badges managed to appear on many vehicles for some years to follow. During this period only Clydesdales and Vikings were built, principally for export. Manufacture of Clydesdales was also undertaken in South Africa during the early 1970s. The resultant vehicles were known as Leyland Elands.

Production of bus chassis at Albion finally ceased in 1980 when the Clydesdale and Viking were moved to Leyland's factory at Bathgate. The Albion factory continues in use as a component assembly plant.

Left: A 1927 Albion PM28 for Leon on Finningley, seen prior to delivery from Roe's coachbuilding works in Leeds. This acceptably modern vehicle was restricted to 12mph when new. *Charles H. Roe*

The Early Days

Before and after World War 1 many Albion goods chassis were bodied as buses. But in September 1923 a new purpose-built bus chassis, the model 24 was announced. This was derived from the contemporary 25 and 30cwt goods chassis but had improved springing. It featured a straight frame; solid, pneumatic or cushion tyres; and a new four-speed gearbox. A four-cylinder engine of 24hp was fitted and six models were advertised suitable for bodywork of various seating capacities between 12 and 23.

A 14ft wheelbase Viking chassis was introduced early in 1924 and found a role as a charabanc in many fleets. This too had a four-cylinder engine and pneumatic tyres. At the end of 1924 the familiar angular outline radiator was introduced on bus models. A variety of 24 series models was now available ranging from the diminutive PA24 (10ft 9in wheelbase) through the PB24 and PC24 (11ft 3in); and PE24 (12ft 9in) to the PF24 and PH24 (14ft). The smallest seated 12; the largest 21. All were of normal-control layout.

A more powerful range, the 30/60hp drop-frame 26 series, joined the 24 series in October 1925. Again there was a variety of wheelbases — from 11ft 3in to 16ft.

In 1927 the first forward-control chassis appeared. This used the 30/60hp engine of the 26 series and was called the Viking PM28. Up to 32 seats could be fitted in this 16ft 3in wheelbase chassis. This same wheelbase was used for a normal-control chassis — the PNA26 — which appeared around the same time, while front wheel brakes were introduced on the PFB26. By the start of 1930 all Viking 26 and 28 series chassis shared a 16ft 3in wheelbase. The forward-control models were the PMA28 (four-cylinder, 60bhp) and PMB28 (six-cylinder, 90bhp). Normal-control variants were the four-cylinder PKA26 and six-cylinder PKB26. Six-cylinder Vikings were known as Viking Sixes. The Vikings were phased out in 1931/2.

Below: West Bromwich Albion. The first motor buses operated by West Bromwich Corporation were these two chain-driven Albions. They entered service on 10 September 1914 and the chassis were then promptly commandeered by the army in October. *Ian Allan Library*

Above: An early postwar charabanc, still chain-driven, but now with the Albion name cast prominently on the radiator top tank. It belorged to a Stirlingshire operator. His customers on this occassion do not look as if they are particularly enjoying their outing!
Stewart J. Brown collection

Below: Massey bodywork of simple design was fitted to this early 1920s demonstrator which was based on a light truck chassis. *R. Marshall collection*

Above: The rebodying of a 10-year old chassis was uncommon in the 1930s when bus design was evolving very rapidly. This 1925 Viking is shown here in 1935 with a new 20-seat coach body by Roberts of Wakefield. It belonged to Bowen of Musselburgh, who sold out to SMT in May 1935. SMT sold the bus in 1936, despite its brand new body. *Roberts*

Below: A more typical Viking is this 1926 example owned by Alexander's of Falkirk. The radiator was of a design introduced on this model. *Stewart J. Brown collection*

Top left: An early bus in the Pretoria Municipal Transport fleet. This is a model 26 of the mid-1920s with locally built bodywork. The angular radiator set the style for future Albions.
R. L. Grieves collection

Centre left: This 1926 PK26 was new to J. & R. Young of Paisley, the predecessors of Young's Bus Service which became a major Albion customer. It was destroyed by fire before the formation of YBS — but was rebuilt and saw further service with an operator in Forfar. *A. J. Douglas collection*

Below: Baillie Brothers of Dumbarton purchased this PJ26 in 1927. It was sold to Alexander's in 1933 and converted from a normal control 25-seater to a forward control 36-seater. The radiator is surmounted by a prominent temperature warning device.
Harry Hay collection

Below: West Lothian Motor Services of Edinburgh owned two of these model 26 chassis with 26-seat Strachans bodies. They were new in January 1929 and joined the SMT fleet when West Lothian was taken over in September of the same year. After four years in service they were sold for conversion to lorries. *Strachans*

Bottom: A PM28 with Mumford body running for the The Valleys Motor Bus Services, one of the predecessors of Red & White. It was new in 1927. *C. Carter*

Above: Grimsby Corporation purchased this long-lived PM28 in 1927 and finally withdrew it in 1955. In this postwar view it has acquired a truck-style radiator top tank. The 32-seat body was built by Roe. *Don Morris*

Below: King Alfred of Winchester operated this PMA28 with rear-entrance Strachans bodywork. *J. F. Higham*

Above: Roe 32-seat bodywork was chosen by Albion for this 1928 PM28 demonstrator. The driving position of this type of Albion can be seen clearly, with its high set steering wheel. Note the destination screen mounted under the front canopy and the location of the entrance door a short distance behind the front bulkhead. *Charles H. Roe*

Below: The six-cylinder PMB28 — or Viking Six — had its radiator located further forward. This is one of two demonstrators which were purchased by the General Omnibus Company of Dublin. When the General was acquired by Dublin United Tramways in late 1934 its fleet included 22 Albions. *Albion*

Valkyrie

At the end of 1930 the PX65 was announced. This was a forward-control chassis with a 16ft 3in wheelbase and a 60bhp 5 litre four-cylinder engine. Designed to carry 32-seat bodywork it was given the type name Valkyrie. During 1931 the PW65 was introduced; it had a 17ft 8in wheelbase and could carry 36 seated passengers.

A 6.1 litre four-cylinder petrol engine was introduced in 1933 in the PW67, which replaced the 65 series models, and in 1934 the 39-seat PW69 was announced. Interest in oil engines was increasing at this time and Valkyries were made available with Albion, Beardmore or Gardner oil engines if operators requested them. The prefix letters SP (for special) usually indicated an oil engined chassis.

New Valkyries appeared in 1935. The PW141 retained the 80bhp engine of its predecessors while the PV141 had a 110bhp six-cylinder 7.8 litre unit as used in the Valiant which it soon replaced. Most Valkyries were used as coaches and Albion continued to list petrol engines as standard when most other manufacturers saw diesel as standard and petrol as an option. In the 141-series Valkyries customers could have oil engines of Albion or Gardner manufacture.

Two short-lived three-axle Valkyrie models were introduced in 1936. The PR145 had the 80bhp four-cylinder engine which was compact enough to allow 44-seat bodywork to be fitted. The PW145 used the 110bhp six-cylinder unit.

Below: New in December 1930, this was an early 65-series Valkyrie for W. Alexander & Sons of Falkirk. It had operator-built 30-seat bodywork. *Albion*

Above: Four Roberts-bodied Valkyries ready for delivery to MacShanes for use on Liverpool local services. The grant of licences to MacShanes for these services was quickly rescinded and the vehicles passed to the Red & White group which had been involved in their purchase. *Roberts*

Centre right: A 1931 PW65 of Young's Bus Service heads a fascinating line of vehicles in Glasgow's Clyde Street. *Stewart J. Brown collection*

Bottom right: Hebble was a fairly loyal Albion customer until World War II. This Brush-bodied PW65 was delivered in 1932. *Brush*

Above: With its radiator mounted further forward than on earlier models, the PW67 was an altogether more modern looking vehicle. This Willowbrook-bodied example, seen in the livery of Dodds of Troon, was originally an Albion demonstrator. *A. J. Douglas collection*

Below: Nicely-proportioned English Electric 32-seat bodywork was fitted to this PW67 of South Yorkshire, the independent operator based in Pontefract. It was new in 1934 and ended its days rebuilt as a forward entrance service bus. *G. H. F. Atkins*

Below: This bizarrely streamlined Valkyrie PW69 was new in 1935 to an Australian operator, United Motors. It had a Syd Wood body. *Albion*

Bottom: Postwar bodywork by Walker of Aberdeen helps conceal the age of this 1936 Valkyrie PW69. It was owned by Strachan's Deeside Omnibus Service of Ballater and is seen here in Aberdeen.
Stewart J. Brown collection

Above: A Valkyrie of BEST — the Bombay Electricity Supply and Transport Company — advertising limited stop services in the late 1930s. The cutaway rear platform is reminiscent of contemporary Scottish practice.
Ian Allan Library

Left: Highland Omnibuses acquired this PW141 from its predecessor, the Highland Transport Company. New in 1937, it ran until 1957. The 32-seat Cowieson body has been extensively rebuilt by Highland Transport.
Stewart J. Brown collection

Bottom left: The most impressive Valkyries were 15 three-axle PW145s delivered to Young's of Paisley in 1937/38. They had 39-seat Cowieson bodywork and were fairly short-lived. This one was sold in 1946 to Ansell's Coaches which was the first of three South London owners of the vehicle. It is seen running on hire to London Transport.
Stewart J. Brown collection

Valiant

Valiant was one of the less common Albion model names. Late in 1931 the PV70 was introduced with a 6.03 litre 85bhp six-cylinder petrol engine. This Valiant was a forward-control chassis with a 17ft 4in wheelbase and was designed to take 36-seat bodywork. It was therefore bigger than the Viking Six and more powerful than the Valkyrie.

In 1935 a change of engine produced the PV71. This had the 7.8 litre engine fitted to the Valkyrie PV141 or the option of a Gardner 5LW. The Valiant was dropped in 1936, ousted by the successful range of Valkyries.

Below: The Valiant had a heavier-looking radiator than its contemporaries, helping to give it an appearance of power. This PV70 was delivered to Hebble in 1934 and had a luxurious Northern Counties coach body. It ran until 1949.
Northern Counties

Above: Tourist Motor Coaches (Southampton) Ltd ran a number of Albions including this Valiant with Strachans coach body which had an oddly-positioned doorway in the second bay and a roof luggage compartment. *Strachans*

Centre left: Sleek Duple bodywork was specified by Fallowfield & Knight for this rear-entrance Valiant coach. The valance above the front wing is hinged at the front pillar so that it does not impede access to the engine. The roof rack is reached by steps in the pillar ahead of the door, in contrast with Strachans who provided a ladder on the back of the body. This Valiant must have been a very fine coach. *Duple*

Bottom left: Red & White bought three PV71s in 1935; this one with rather heavy-looking bodywork is seen at Cheltenham coach station. *J. F. Higham*

Victor

The PH49 was introduced in 1930 and was a normal control chassis with a 14ft 6in wheelbase. Power was provided by a 42bhp 3.15 litre four-cylinder engine. Designed as a 20-seater it replaced the PH24. A 60bhp 3.62 litre engine soon replaced the original unit and in 1933 the PH49 was joined by the bigger PHA49 and PHC49, while in 1934 it was superseded by the PHB49. The 26-seat PH111 was produced for a short time in 1934.

In 1934 the Victor received a new engine of 3.89 litre capacity. This engine developed 65bhp and the new Victors formed the 115 series. The PH115 was a forward-control chassis with the 14ft 6in wheelbase of the original Victor. The PK115 was a forward-control machine with a 16ft 4in wheelbase. Two further Victors appeared in 1934: the PH114 (14ft 6in wheelbase) and the PK114 (17ft 2in wheelbase). Both were of normal-control layout.

The majority of Victors was sold to coach operators and the model faded from the scene with the outbreak of war in 1939.

Below: A 1932 49-series Victor alongside a 1935 PK115 in the fleet of Ferguson of Renfrew who traded as Victor Bus Service. The older normal control vehicle was bodied by Cadogan of Perth while the PK115 had a Cowieson body. Note the different styles of radiators. Ferguson operated between Paisley and Renfrew Ferry.
R. L. Grieves collection

Top: McAdoo of Cudworth bought this attractive 30-seat PK115 in 1935. It demonstrates the Victor's scaled-down 'big bus' appearance.
G. R. Mills collection

Above: A neat little Victor with bodywork by Park of Glasgow, built in 1935 for Glasgow Corporation Education Department who remained a loyal Albion customer until the 1950s. A Leyland advertising sign is just visible on the wall to the right of the photograph — prophetic?
R. L. Grieves collection

Above: Cronshaw of Hendon owned this Victor PK115 with locally-built Duple bodywork. It was exhibited by Albion at the 1937 Earls Court show and weighed a mere 4¼ tons unladen. It was a 26-seater. *Albion*

Right: The later normal-control models featured the less angular radiator shown on this PK114 with Abbot body which was new in 1935 to King Alfred of Winchester. It is seen here beside the famous King Alfred statue. *D. Hurley*

Venturer

The Venturer was Albion's first double-deck chassis. The Model 80 was announced at the end of 1932 and had a 16ft 3in wheelbase and a 6.85 litre six-cylinder petrol engine. A Gardner oil engine was available as an option. In 1933 it was offered with a 6.98 litre petrol engine.

The early Venturers could hold up to 51 seats — the Venturer 81 launched in 1935 could accommodate 55 seats and had a Gardner 6LW oil engine as standard. The Albion 7.8 litre 103bhp petrol engine used in the Valiant and Valkyrie was available as an option. While six-wheeled single-deckers retained the name of the model from which they were derived. Albion's six-wheel double-deck chassis was given a new name — Valorous 85. In the event, only one was built using the 7.8 litre EN85 engine which was later fitted to the Valkyrie PV141.

Below: An early Venturer demonstrator with 48-seat Northern Counties bodywork. It was built in 1933 and was later sold to Alexander's of Falkirk in whose livery it is seen. The general outline of radiator and bonnet altered little during 20 years of Venturer production. *Albion*

Above: A Gardner-engined 80-series Venturer in the fleet of Young's Bus Service of Paisley. It had a 48-seat Northern Counties body and was new in 1934, at which time Young's fleet was entirely of Albion manufacture.
A. J. Douglas collection

Centre right: The M81 Venturer was designed to carry 55 passengers, which was the capacity of this example delivered to Young's in 1936. It had a Gardner 6LW engine. Young's business was acquired by Western SMT in 1951 and this vehicle is one of four M81s which ran for Western until 1955. It had a Northern Counties body. *S. N. J. White*

Bottom right: The one and only three-axle Albion double-decker was this 1932 Valorous. It was built as a demonstrator, sold to Young's of Paisley in 1933, and ended its days with a showman by whom it was purchased in 1944. It seated 60 passengers.
A. J. Douglas collection

Valkyrie CX

At the 1937 Commercial Motor Show, the first to be held at Earls Court, Albion's CX range of chassis was unveiled. The CX models had the engine and gearbox mounted as a single unit, a feature previously seen only on the lightweight Victor chassis. There were three new Valkyries. The CX9 had the 6.1 litre four-cylinder petrol engine developed from that first seen in the PW67 in 1933 and carried over to the PW141. The CX11 had Gardner's 7.0 litre 5LW oil engine. The CX13 had a new 9.1 litre six-cylinder petrol engine, with the 8.4 litre Gardner 6LW as an option. An Albion oil engine, developed from the petrol engine, was soon available in the CX9 and returned excellent fuel consumption figures: one contemporary test reported 15.7mpg. The Gardner 4LW was also fitted to the CX9.

Valkyrie production was halted by the war but resumed in 1945 with the CX9 and the CX13 having diesel engines as standard and petrol engines as an option. The CX9 now had a 6.6 litre four-cylinder unit while the CX13 had the 9.1 litre Albion diesel; both had a 17ft 7in wheelbase, a figure unchanged since the introduction of the CX range.

Valkyrie production ceased in 1950.

Below: An early Valkyrie CX11 in the Red & White fleet. The last two digits in the fleet number in this postwar view show that it was new in 1937. The bodywork was by Duple.
Don Morris

Below: A prewar CX13 chassis with a postwar Burlingham coach body in the South Yorkshire fleet. The body was removed from a Valiant CX39 which South Yorkshire had rebodied as a double-decker. *G. R. Mills*

Bottom: Red & White stayed loyal to the Albion/Gardner/ Duple combination. This CX11 of 1939 has a centre-entrance bus body. *J. F. Higham*

Above: A petrol-engined Valkyrie CX13 of South African Railways in 1940. Albion's original caption implies that the vehicle behind is a Venturer, some of which were also being supplied to SAR — but it is in fact a Leyland Titan TD5!
Albion

Below: A 1946 CX13 with diesel engine and Pickering body, photographed before delivery to a member of A1 Service, the Ayrshire co-operative. Note the location of the entrance doors at the top of the steps, a layout favoured by a minority of coachbuilders and operators. The flashes on the side are a brave attempt to soften the utilitarian lines of the body.
Albion

Below: Between 1952 and 1954 Brislington Body Works fitted Eastern Coach Works-style bodies to 15 1947 Valkyrie CX13s in the Red & White fleet. When new they had smart — albeit not very durable — Pickering forward-entrance bodies. Their new BBW bodies were of rear-entrance layout as shown in this bleak November view among the prefabs of Troedrhiwgwair. The advert on the cove panels for sightseeing tours seem a bit out of place! *R. A. Mills, A. Moyes*

Above: A handsome Duple-bodied Valkyrie in the fleet of Ribbeck of Brodick on the Isle of Arran collects steamer passengers at Lochranza Pier in 1965. *Stewart J. Brown*

Below: A four-cylinder CX9 which was new in 1948 to Macrae & Dick of Inverness. One of a pair, it had bodywork by Brockhouse of Clydebank. Macrae & Dick became part of Highland Omnibuses in 1951 and this photograph shows the bus in Highland's maroon and cream livery in the early 1950s. Both buses were sold by Highland in 1959.
Stewart J. Brown collection

COLEFORD
VIA
TINTERN
S548
GWO 866
2
PONTYPOOL
BLACKWOOD

DEPOT
249
249
HANSON
DVH821

Left: A 1948 CX13 of Red & White with Lydney bodywork which bears a strong resemblance to contemporary Guy products with its outswept skirt panels, radiused window corners and shallow top-sliding ventilators. *A. J. Douglas*

Bottom left: The Hanson of Huddersfield fleet included this 1949 Valkyrie with attractive Duple 35-seat bus body. It was withdrawn in 1962. *T. W. W. Knowles*

Below: A fine line up of new Brockhouse-bodied Valkyries — five for the Gold Coast, one for the Clyde coast. Despite the vastly different operating conditions, the vehicles for Africa are remarkably similar to that for Scotland. The bus nearest the camera was for A1 Service of Ardrossan. *R. L. Grieves collection*

Bottom: This 1950 CX13 was acquired by Chesterfield Corporation early in 1960 with the business of F. H. Doughty of Birmington. The 35-seat body was by Street. *R. Marshall*

Venturer CX

The Venturer CX19 was announced in 1937, along with the Valkyrie CX range. The CX19 had an Albion 9.1 litre oil engine as standard, with Gardner's 6LW oil or Albion petrol engines available as options.

Production of the CX19 recommenced after the war. In 1947 it was superseded by the CX37 which had a 9.9 litre Albion diesel developing 120bhp compared with the 105bhp of the smaller engine used in the CX19. The last petrol-engined Venturers were built in 1948 for South African Railways and were the last petrol-engined double-deckers built in Britain. The last CX37 chassis was built in 1951, just before Albion was taken over by Leyland.

Below and right: A 1938 Venturer CX19 with English Electric body, seen prior to delivery to Young's of Paisley. It was one of four which were rebodied in 1953 by Eastern Coach Works, after the Young's business had been taken over by Western SMT. The same vehicle is seen in Dumfries after rebodying. These vehicles had Gardner engines.
GEC Traction, R. Marshall

Above: As late as 1941 quite well-appointed double-deckers were still being delivered to Red & White. This is a CX19 with lowbridge Duple bodywork. Note the headlamp masks and white paint on the wing tips, lifeguards and platform edge.
Ian Allan Library

Right: The New South Wales Department of Road Transport & Tramways was the biggest postwar Venturer customer, buying 143 between 1947 and 1949. This is a 1947 SPCX19W with 59-seat Commonwealth Engineering body. The last Venturer was withdrawn in 1971 by the Department of Government Transport which had succeeded the DRTT in 1952. *John Ward*

Below: From New South Wales to old South Wales. Until it was purchased by the British Transport Commission Red & White stayed loyal to Albion. This 1948 CX19 has angular bodywork by Welsh Metal Industries of Caerphilly.
J. F. Higham

Above: A smaller but no less loyal customer was South Yorkshire of Pontefract. This Venturer had lowbridge bodywork by Strachans. *R. Marshall*

Centre left: Two CX19s of United Welsh — part of the Red & White empire — in Neath in 1958. Both were new in 1948 and had Eastern Coach Works bodies. The sunrise motif cast in the radiator of the vehicle on the left is unusual; most later Venturers had the simpler casting seen on the bus on the right. *Ian Allan Library*

Bottom left: The first new double-deckers to be purchased by Bedwas & Machen Urban District Council were two CX19 Venturers. New in 1948 they had all-aluminium bodies by Welsh Metal Industries. The second one, which was withdrawn in 1961, is seen here after being rebuilt with rubber mounted windows. Bedwas & Machen was one of the constituents of Rhymney Valley District Council which was created in 1974. *R. L. Wilson*

Above: A CX19 in Hyderabad surrounded by bicycles — often a major competitor for public transport in developing countries. Albions sold fairly well in India, but were usually single-decked. *Albion*

Left: Albion double-deckers never featured prominently in SMT group fleets. This Venturer CX37 was one of 16 purchased by Western SMT in 1949. They had lowbridge Alexander bodywork. *J. M. Aldridge*

Above right: The British-style double-decker appears incongruous in the American-style surroundings of central Johannesburg. These CX37s for South African Railways were the last petrol-engined double-deckers built in Britain. They had 30ft long six-bay bodywork by Bus Bodies (South Africa). *Albion*

Right: Five Metro-Cammell-bodied CX19s joined the Cheltenham District fleet in 1949 and were generally similar to 24 vehicles supplied to Glasgow Corporation in the previous year. This view was taken in The Promenade, Cheltenham. *R. F. Mack*

EMPIRE CYCLE CO. LTD
HUMBER
CYCLES
COLOSSEUM
TG10398

WARDEN HILL
6
SCRAP!
WEIGH YOURS IN ON
THE BAILEY BRIDGE
LTD.
HDG444

Victor FT

The Victor name was revived in 1947 for a model similar in spirit but different in concept from its prewar namesake. The FT series Victor was still a lightweight chassis — but it had a straight frame to enable it to cope with poor roads in export markets. Many Victors saw service in rural parts of Africa.

The first model, the FT3AB, had an 80bhp 4.26 litre Albion six-cylinder petrol engine. In 1948 it was joined by the FT39 which had a four cylinder 75bhp 4.88 litre Albion diesel engine. The FT3AB was withdrawn in 1951. In the following year the FT39AN (16ft wheelbase) and FT39AL (16ft 11½in wheelbase, were introduced and were by then the only passenger chassis available from Albion.

The 5.48 litre four-cylinder EN287 diesel engine was fitted in 1956 and the Victor models became the FT39KAN and FT39KAL. By this time virtually all Victors were exported. The FT range of Victors was replaced by the VT range in 1959.

Below: An entirely Scottish Albion. Bodywork by Scottish Aviation of Prestwick was fitted to this FT39N operated by Kyle Brothers of Kelso. It is seen in Kelso market place in 1964, loading for Greatridgehall. *R. L. Iles*

Above: Most Victors had exposed radiators with the large sunrise motif on the top tank. This example, with a coach body by James Whitson & Co of Yiewsley, was operated by Whites of Camberley, a long-standing Albion user in Surrey. *Ian Allan Library*

Centre left: An FT39N, new in 1951 to Beeston of East Bergholt, with a 31-seat Thurgood body. Beeston's business was taken over by Eastern Counties later in 1951. This Victor was acquired for preservation by Geoff Mills of Colchester. *G. R. Mills*

Bottom left: A petrol-engined FT3AB which was supplied to Skye Transport, part of the Scottish Cooperative Wholesale Society, in 1952. The Skye Transport business was taken over in 1958 by MacBrayne, which ran this bus until 1966. It had bodywork by Harvey of Strathaven. *A. J. Douglas*

Above: It was not only the smaller bodybuilders who bodied Victors. This FT39L had an Eastern Coach Works body. It was new in 1953 and was the last rear-entrance single-decker to be purchased by Eastern Counties. This view of it reversing into Eye depot was taken in 1965. *G. R. Mills*

Below: Duple coach bodies of a style generally associated with Bedford SB chassis were fitted to some Victors. This 1955 FT39 is seen in Inverness bus station in 1967, shortly after acquisition by Highland Omnibuses. It was previously operated by Seaforth MacGregor of Dornoch.
Stewart J. Brown

Below: Strachans Everest bodywork is fitted to this 1955 FT39 which was operated by Lowland Motorways of Glasgow. It is seen outside Renfrew Airport operating the service to British European Airways' Glasgow office. Now all have gone — Lowland taken over by Scottish Omnibuses; Renfrew Airport replaced by Glasgow Airport; BEA absorbed by British Airways; and the Victor to the scrapyard. *Albion*

Bottom: Guernsey was for many years a steady market for small Albions. This Victor FT39AN was delivered to the Guernsey Railway Company in 1955 and still looked very smart when photographed 23 years later. It had a 35-seat Heaver body. *G. R. Mills*

Top: Harrington and Albion were a standard combination at Charlie's Cars of Bournemouth. This is a 1956 Victor — wearing a livery which obviously dated from an earlier era.
A. D. Broughall

Above: Where traffic has not justified a railway line many railway administrations have chosen to run buses. This fleet of Victors is typical of many sold in Africa and belonged to the East African Railways & Harbours Board which in 1958 operated them in Tanganyika (now Tanzania). Note the roof luggage racks. *EAR&H*

Valiant CX39

The Valiant CX39 was introduced in 1948 to replace the CX13 Valkyrie and was powered by the 120bhp engine used in the double-deck Venturer CX37. The Valiant thus complemented the four-cylinder CX9 Valkyrie which was rated at 78bhp. Most Valiants were fitted with coach bodywork and the model was withdrawn in 1951.

Above left: Dye of Hereford owned this 1949 Valiant with 35-seat Thurgood body. In this view it is still in service with its original owner, despite being 16 years old. *G. R. Mills*

Left: Economic of Whitburn specified bodywork by Associated Coach Builders of Sunderland for this Valiant in 1950. *G. Coxon*

Above: This Valiant CX39 with Duple body was part of a batch of 13 delivered to Red & White in 1950 which were to be the last Albions purchased. 1950 was the year in which Red & White was purchased by the British Transport Commission. *J. M. Aldridge*

Centre right: Blue Bus Service of Slough operated this ex-Easson of Southampton Valiant which is seen outside Windsor Castle in 1964. It had a Reading body and was new in 1950. *G. R. Mills*

Bottom right: Not quite what it seems! This 'Venturer' of South Yorkshire started life as a Burlingham-bodied Valiant. In 1957 it received this new 53-seat Roe body, thus becoming the last genuine (ie pre-Leyland) Albion in Britain to receive a new body. Its original coach body was transferred to a prewar Valkyrie chassis. *G. R. Mills*

Viking CX41/HD61

The Viking model, announced in 1948, was intended primarily for the export market and was fitted with the 120bhp 9.91 litre engine used in the Venturer CX37 and Valiant CX39. The straight-framed CX41 was offered with 18ft 3in and 20ft 6in wheelbases and had a four-speed gearbox as standard.

Two years later, in 1950, a new Viking was announced in 19ft and 21ft wheelbase versions. This, the HD61, had a five-speed gearbox. But this Viking was shortlived — by 1952 production had ceased.

Below: The postwar Viking HD61N was a comparatively rare beast on the home market. This Thurgood-bodied example was new to Dye of Hertford but is seen here late in its life running on the Isle of Arran for Bannatyne of Blackwaterfoot. *A. J. Douglas*

Below: The massive-looking radiator of the Viking is illustrated by this example owned by Campbell of Pitsea, Essex. It was new in 1951 and had an Allweather body.
R. H. G. Simpson

Underfloor engines

KP71NW

In 1951 the first underfloor-engined bus chassis emerged from Albion's works. This was the experimental KP71NW which had a horizontally-opposed eight-cylinder engine — using basically two four-cylinder EN286 cylinder blocks — of 9.76 litre capacity. A five-speed gearbox was fitted. Only two KP71NW chassis were built. It was perhaps a case of too much, too late. The tide had turned in favour of lightweights.

Nimbus

So Albion produced the lightest of lightweights — the Nimbus. This tiny chassis with 11ft 10in wheelbase appeared at the Scottish Motor Show in November 1955. Designated MR9, it was powered by a four-cylinder 3.83 litre EN219 engine fitted horizontally in the wheelbase This engine was basically two-thirds of the contemporary Leyland O.350 six-cylinder unit.

In 1958 the MR9 was replaced by the NS3 which had the same wheelbase but a 72bhp 4.1 litre EN250 engine. The NS3N was 23ft 3in long and the NS3L was 24ft long. The availability of five or six-speed gearboxes in place of the original four-speed unit produced the NS3AN in 1961. The Nimbus achieved only limited popularity with rural operators, but anticipated the 1970s midibus trend in a few municipal fleets. A small number was exported. Production ceased in 1963.

Aberdonian

The most conventional of Albion's underfloor-engined chassis was the Aberdonian which can perhaps best be described as a sort of lightweight Leyland Tiger Cub. Announced in the summer of 1957 the MR11L had a Leyland O.350 engine rated at 94bhp and a 16ft 4in wheelbase. An Albion five-speed constant mesh gearbox was standard. Sales were not exactly spectacular with most customers buying one batch but not placing repeat orders. Aberdonians found their way to Australia and to Ceylon, where 100 were ordered. The Aberdonian was withdrawn from the market in 1960.

Below: Only two examples of the KP71NW were built and both had bodywork by Scottish Aviation of Prestwick. This one operated on demonstration to Western SMT from 1952 to 1955 before being returned to Albion. The other had a bus body and was used by Glasgow Corporation.
Stewart J. Brown

Above: Highland Omnibuses bought six MR9 Nimbuses (or Nimbii?) in 1956. The first of these demonstrates the ability of small buses to get to areas bigger buses cannot reach. Alexander built the 29-seat body. *Gavin Booth collection*

Centre right: A trio of Aberdonian MR11Ls joined the Western SMT fleet in 1957. All had Alexander bodies, this one being finished as a 39-seater in black and white coach livery. Only 26 Aberdonians were purchased by SMT group companies — those which bought Leyland group single-deckers opted to stay with the Tiger Cub. *Albion*

Bottom right: Manchester Corporation features prominently in the Crossley section of this book but barely merits a mention in relation to Albion. The only Albions ever owned by Manchester were six Aberdonians with 42-seat Seddon bodies. New in 1958 they were used as one-man operated buses; a rare feature in municipal transport at that time. They were sold after 10 years service. *Ian Allan Library*

Above: Venture Transport, the Consett-based independent, bought 17 Aberdonians in 1958/59. Willowbrook 41-seat bodywork is fitted to this 1958 MR11 seen in Consett bus station. *A. D. Broughall*

Below: Hill of Wollongong, New South Wales, operated this 1958 Aberdonian with Cycle Components Manufacturing Co 43-seat body. It weighed only five tons unladen. *Ian Allan Library.*

Top right: The Ceylon Transport Board bought both Aberdonians and Nimbuses. One of the latter, with a locally-built body, is seen when new. The Albion sunrise badge bears a strange interpretation of the Leyland scroll — badge engineering at its most basic! *Ian Allan Library*

Right and below: A few Nimbuses received Plaxton coach bodies. Smith's of Wigan tried them on tours to the Isle of Skye — one is seen here in the 1956 Brighton Coach Rally. A later, and less attractive, coach was delivered to Watson of Harrogate in 1961. Over-ornamentation spoiled the appearance of this centre-entrance 29-seater.
Ian Allan Library, Gavin Booth collection

Above: One of the Ulster Transport Authority's 57 Aberdonians seen when new in 1960. The UTA body was a fairly blatant copy of a contemporary Alexander design but was built on Metsec frames with no Alexander involvement. *R. C. Ludgate collection*

Below: Willowbrook bodied a few Nimbuses including this demonstrator which was later purchased by Barrie's Coaches of Balloch. It is seen in Drymen Square in 1962. *Harry Hay*

Top right: One of six Aberdonians purchased by Charlie's Cars of Bournemouth in 1960. The combination of Harrington body and Aberdonian chassis is unusual — and the application of the Charlie's Cars livery to the well proportioned body verges on the sacrilegious. Charlie's Cars were taken over by Shamrock & Rambler in 1963, which was in turn purchased by Hants & Dorset in 1966. This photograph was taken in Victoria Coach station in 1960. *Gavin Booth*

Centre right: A few British Electric Traction group companies tried the Nimbus. Western Welsh had 48; Maidstone & District ran 15. Less well known were the nine operated by Devon General, three of which were new in 1962 and had Harrington bodywork. This one is seen in 1964 at Ottery St Mary. *A. D. Broughall*

Below: Nimbuses were also operated by a small number of municipalities — Halifax, Great Yarmouth, Southampton and Wallasey. The last named bought four at the end of 1962, all of which survived to be acquired by the Merseyside PTE on its formation in 1969 and were withdrawn in the early 1970s. They were NS3AN models with 31-seat Strachans bodies. *G. R. Mills*

Victor VT

A new range of front-engined Victors appeared in 1959. The VT15 was fitted with the 5.48 litre four-cylinder diesel used in the FT39 but in a modified form known as the EN289. The VT17 had a vertical Leyland O.350 six-cylinder unit. Two wheelbases were listed — 15ft 6in and 17ft 3in and these were denoted by the suffix N or L after the chassis designation. Minor engineering modifications saw the change in 1960 to VT15A (with EN335 engine) and VT17A. When the Leyland O.370 engine was installed in the Victor in 1962 it became the VT17B. These, like the FT series which had preceded them, were aimed primarily at export markets.

An attempt was made to regain lost home market business and to cover a gap in Leyland's range by introducing the VT21L in 1962. This had a 17ft $8\frac{1}{2}$in wheelbase and an O.370 engine but was not a success in a market which was dominated by Bedford. Production of the VT series Victor ceased in 1966, its place in export markets being taken by the new Viking.

Below: A minority of early 1960s Victors were bodied by Plaxton. This one for Lawrenson's of Bootle is in pristine condition for the 1963 National Coach Rally in Blackpool.
M. Fowler

Above: The Duple Firefly body had attractive lines and was chosen by Albion for its VT21L demonstration coach in 1964. Victor coaches were generally 41-seaters. *Stewart J. Brown*

Below: Typifying Albion's involvement in basic buses for overseas use is this Victor VT17 for Boston Transport of Barbados. The 35-seat two-door body was by Mulliner. The truck-style front end makes an interesting comparison with the contemporary Lowlander. This bus was new in 1962. *Albion*

Clydesdale

The Clydesdale was essentially a truck range but in 1959 Albion announced the availability of the CD23 for bus use. The CD23NW had a 17ft 6in wheelbase and the CD23LW had a wheelbase of 19ft 1in. Both models were powered by the Leyland 0.375 engine mounted vertically at the front of the chassis and driving through a choice of five or six-speed manual gearboxes. Towards the end of 1960 the CD23A with Leyland 0.400 engine replaced the original model and in 1962 the CD25 was introduced with a set-back front axle allowing a front entrance. Further refinements brought the CD27 (pneumocyclic gearbox) and the CD29 (0.600 engine and pneumocyclic gearbox). The Clydesdale was sold principally to East African operators and continued in production throughout the 1970s. In its final form it was offered only as the ECD23 with 140bhp Leyland 402 engine and Albion five-speed synchromesh gearbox.

Below: Proof that Albions serve both hemispheres — a 1969 Clydesdale CD31 of the Uganda Transport Company about to cross the line of the equator in 1972. It had a locally-built 65-seat bus body with three-and-two seating. The Albion badge still features a sun ray motif. *Stewart J. Brown*

Bottom: Seen in Kampala bus terminal on its first day in service in 1971 is a Clydesdale CD23 coach of East African Road Services. Note the Leyland lettering on the front. EARS was based in Nairobi, whence this vehicle operated the 400-mile trip to Kampala. It carries two registrations — one for Kenya the other for Uganda. The striking livery was black and white and the body was built in Nairobi. *Stewart J. Brown*

Lowlander

Albion's last double-deck model was announced in 1961. Introduced primarily to meet the requirements of the Scottish Bus Group it was intended to be a lowheight equivalent of the contemporary Leyland Titan and had a drop-centre rear axle. All Lowlanders had an 18ft 6in wheelbase. Four models were listed: the LR1 had a pneumocyclic gearbox and the LR3 had a synchromesh gearbox. The LR5 and LR7 were equivalents of the LR1 and LR3 but with air suspension on the rear axle. The Lowlander was fitted with the Leyland O.600 9.8 litre engine. In England it was marketed as a Leyland. The last Lowlanders entered service in 1966.

Right: The Lowlander sold principally to Scottish Bus Group subsidiaries who between them bought 194. Of these, 30 went to Central SMT in 1962/63 including 20 LR1s with Northern Counties bodies which quite effectively disguised the Lowlander's high driving position. Central's Lowlanders were redistributed among other SBG subsidiaries in 1965.
Stewart J. Brown

Below: In contrast, the Alexander body seemed to emphasise the driving position and the front offside upper deck passengers were perched high on top of the cab. English Lowlanders — this is one of 10 Southend LR7s — had Leyland lettering on the grille. *Stewart J. Brown*

Viking VK

Viking was the first name used by Albion for a bus chassis and by fortuitous coincidence the last bus chassis to come from the factory at Scotstoun were destined to have the same name. The VK41 was introduced in 1963. This had a 16ft 1in wheelbase, set-back front axle, and a Leyland O.370 engine mounted vertically at the front of the frame. In general layout it anticipated the Bedford VAM and Ford R series. Very few front-engined Vikings were sold on the home market but the model sold well in many traditional Albion markets overseas, including the Far East and parts of Africa. Over the years a variety of Vikings has come and gone.

The VK55 had a 401 engine and full air brakes (the VK41 had air hydraulic brakes). Short and long VK55s were built ranging from the 12ft 5in wheelbase EVK55CY to the 20ft VK55CUL.

The VK43 appeared in the summer of 1965 and turned the Viking concept back-to-front — it had a vertically-mounted 400 engine at the rear. It retained a straight frame and had a 16ft 2in wheelbase. Home market models were sold principally to the Scottish Bus Group but, as with the front-engined Viking, export sales were significant and the VK43 developed into the VK45 with tropical cooling; the VK49 with pneumocyclic gearbox; the VK57 with Turner gearbox; and the VK67 with full air braking. The front-engined Viking is still in production for overseas markets, now using the same power train as the Clydesdale, but mounted in a lighter frame.

Below: Very few front-engined Vikings ran for British operators. The first was a 1963 Scottish Motor Show exhibit. It had a 41-seat Alexander Y-type body and was painted in the livery of Alexander (Midland) for whom it ran briefly in the autumn of 1964. It ended its days with a Hebridean operator. *Alexander*

Above: Albion's pre-show publicity picture features a heavily retouched AEC Reliance of Scottish Omnibuses' 1963 delivery and offers an interesting comparison with the real thing (previous page). The faked photograph might have looked more convincing if the AEC instrument binnacle had been painted out. *Albion*

Below: This luxurious rear-engined Viking VK43L was exhibited at the 1965 Scottish Motor Show and was one of five operated in 1966/67 by Central SMT in its unusual two-tone blue coach livery. It had an Alexander Y-type body; most other Scottish Bus Group Vikings were 40-seat dual-purpose vehicles. *Albion*

Left: Leyland made an unsuccessful attempt to exploit the coach market with the combination of rear-engined Viking chassis and Park Royal Royalist coach body. The crisp Park Royal body was ahead of its time but conservative coach operators steered clear of this strange alliance of Leyland group products. Illustrated are a 1967 vehicle in the fleet of Red House of Coventry and a demonstration coach.
M. Fowler, Gavin Booth collection

Below: In 1967 Jersey Motor Transport bought four VK41s with 41-seat bodywork by Pennine Coachcraft. This one is seen at St Aubin in 1977. *G. R. Mills*

Top: Not quite in the Albion image of basic buses for export is this 36ft long rear-engined Viking for Sampson's Tours of New South Wales. It has 41 seats. *Leyland*

Below: As late as 1978 a few Vikings were still being supplied in the home market. This EVK55CL has an Alexander (Belfast) body with 45 glass fibre seats and was for the Northern Ireland Southern Education & Library Board.
Charles Hurst (Commercials) Ltd

Specials

More than most manufacturers, Albion has a long history of making truck chassis available for bus use or of developing special truck-derived chassis to meet customers' special requirements, especially in developing countries where operating conditions can be particularly arduous.

During the 1920s and 1930s some of the smaller goods chassis were bodied as buses. In more recent times (1958) the Royal Scot was built for South African Railways with a 15.2 litre engine mounted in a three axle chassis.

Albion's expertise in building small vehicles has been used at home by Scottish Omnibuses which built an integral bus in 1956 based on Claymore truck components and by Bristol which used the Nimbus engine in its own small chassis, the SU.

Below: Corcoran of Tadcaster purchased this Roberts-bodied LB40 lorry chassis in May 1929. Note the radiator top tank which is of a style not normally seen on buses. The paintwork on the 16-seat body is carefully lined out. *Roberts*

Top right: A slightly bigger truck chassis formed the basis of this 1933 bus destined for operation in Iraq. It has Gruss air springs on the front axle. For services using rough roads the high chassis frame of a truck minimises problems with ground clearance. *Albion*

Centre right: In the mid-1930s 10 of these P56 chassis were supplied to South African Railways. They were designed for fast operation over unmade roads and had petrol engines. The setting is Cape Town harbour with the outline of Table Mountain in the background. *R. L. Grieves collection*

Below: Many truck-based Albion buses have run in Africa but few could have been as impressive as this mighty three-axle 35ft long South African Railways machine. It could carry five first class, nine second class and an unspecified (or unlimited!) number of third class passengers. It could tow a luggage trailer and has a coupling in front of the radiator to help when manouevering the trailer. It could also act as a posting box — the slot for letters is just visible below the fleet number at the front nearside corner. The bodywork was built by Bus Bodies (South Africa) and the bus entered service in 1954. *Ian Allan Library*

Helping Glasgow Flourish

Above: Glasgow's first Albions were PM28s with Cowieson bodies which, like the chassis, were a local product. Two were purchased in 1927, followed in March 1928 by the 10 shown here outside Albion's offices. None ran for more than four years, a short life even by the standards of that time. *R. L. Grieves collection*

Centre left: This M80 was an early Venturer demonstrator. New in 1932 it was never owned by Glasgow Corporation. It joined the fleet of Young's Bus Service in nearby Paisley in 1933. *R. Marshall collection*

Bottom left: The next Albions to be purchased were 50 Venturer 81s with Cowieson bodywork. Twenty Gardner-engined SP81s were delivered in 1935 followed by 30 Beardmore-engined M81s in 1936. An M81 is seen on hire to London Transport in 1940 with the National Gallery in the background. *London Transport*

Top right: In 1938 the first of 80 prewar CX19s were delivered. The 1938 delivery — of which this is one — consisted of 15 Cowieson-bodied 56-seaters with appropriate BUS registrations. *R. Marshall*

Centre right: All 20 of the 1939 delivery of CX19s plus 10 later vehicles were rebodied as shown here by East Lancashire Coachbuilders in 1952. In this form they gave another eight years service. *Stewart J. Brown collection*

Below: In 1942 eight Venturers were bodied in the Corporation's workshops, making use of Metro-Cammell frames. One is seen here nearing completion.
Stewart J. Brown collection

Above: More CX19s were purchased after the war. The first 24, delivered in 1947/48, had Roberts bodywork with a particularly upright front end profile. They were withdrawn in 1960. *A. J. Douglas collection*

Below: The more powerful CX37 was purchased in 1949/50. A total of 65 was bodied by Roberts of Wakefield, Croft of Glasgow, Scottish Aviation of Prestwick or, as shown here, Brockhouse of Clydebank. The location is George Square. *Stewart J. Brown collection*

Above: Glasgow's last Albions were 25 8ft wide CX37SW with Weymann bodywork. These were delivered in 1953 but only lasted for some 10 years. This one is shown in 1957 passing Queen Street station. *R. Marshall*

Centre right: Albion optimistically painted its first Lowlander in Glasgow livery. It was exhibited at the 1961 Scottish Motor Show and is seen here soon after entering service in 1962. It had an Alexander body and by a strange quirk of fate ended its days in the Ribble fleet. Ribble acquired it with the Bamber Bridge Motor Services business.
Gavin Booth

Bottom right: In deference to local feeling Leyland supplied Glasgow with Titans and Atlanteans fitted with Albion badges. A 1962 PDR1/1 with attractive Alexander 78-seat bodywork illustrates the point in Trongate in 1963.
R. L. Wilson

Crossley

Prewar years

Crossley's involvement in the bus chassis business was comparatively brief — only 25 years, from 1928 to 1952. However, the firm's origins go back into the 19th century when Crossley Brothers was a well-established engine manufacturer.

Crossley started building motor cars in 1904 and a new company, Crossley Motors Ltd, was created in 1910. Crossley was based in Gorton, on the eastern side of Manchester. One car model, the 20/25hp, is worthy of mention as this became famous during World War 1 as the basis of a number of military vehicles and after the war 20/25hp chassis were often fitted with bus bodywork.

Car production continued until 1937 (and included an unsuccessful rear-engined model), but it was in 1928 that Crossley unveiled its first proper bus. This was the Eagle, a 5.3 litre 70bhp four-cylinder forward-control single-decker — petrol-engined, of course, at this stage. It had a 16ft $7\frac{1}{2}$in wheelbase, a four-speed sliding mesh gearbox and a neat front end with a parallel-sided radiator mounted by a triangular profile top tank carrying the Maltese cross symbol. Eagle production continued until 1931, by which time almost 80 had been built. A normal-control Eagle was also announced, but only one was actually made.

After a short trial with the first Eagle prototype, Manchester Corporation bought five in 1929, thus starting a 20-year relationship with Crossley. Ironically, Crossley's survival as a bus manufacturer was aided by the depression which encouraged Manchester transport committee to support local industry. Without Manchester's orders it is difficult to see how Crossley could have remained in the bus business.

In 1929 a bigger 110bhp six-cylinder 6.8 litre petrol engine was offered in the same chassis with a similar, but deeper, radiator. This was known as the Crossley Six or Arrow. The Arrow name was also used by Dennis for a single-deck chassis. Dennis presumably had a stronger claim to the name and Crossley renamed its model Alpha. A double-deck version was also called Crossley Six before being named Condor. It first appeared in 1930.

At the same time a small normal-control chassis — the Hawk — was introduced. This had the four-cylinder 5.3 litre engine of the Eagle but in a 15ft 6in wheelbase chassis designed for 26-seat bodywork. Although advertised until 1933 only a dozen were built, all in the 1929-31 period.

The next major Crossley development was the fitting of Gardner 6L2 oil engines to a trio of Condors in 1930. The first of these entered service in Leeds in September and was the country's first diesel-engined double-deck bus. Simultaneously with this development Crossley — with its long experience in engine production — had been designing its own six-cylinder oil engine. This was an 80bhp 9.12 litre direct injection unit and in December 1930 Crossley became the first British manufacturer to offer a complete oil-engined double-deck bus — chassis, engine, gearbox and body.

Oil-engined Condors had a new style of radiator with a shell which was wider at the top than at the bottom and had a less angular appearance with a more pronounced Maltese cross motif. So quick was customer acceptance of oil engines that the last petrol-engined Condors entered service in 1932 and very few petrol-engined Alphas were built after that date. Although the direct injection engine was also offered in the Alpha only two were built, both in 1933. Petrol engines continued to be advertised until 1937,

At the beginning of 1932 a six-wheel double-deck chassis was advertised, powered by the 9.12 litre direct injection oil engine and costing £1,850. (A Condor cost £1,200 with a petrol engine or £1,500 with a diesel.) One six-wheel chassis was built but failed to find a buyer and was eventually sold with a partly built body to Manchester Corporation. It entered service at the end of 1934 and remained unique. No other three-axle motorbuses were built by Crossley.

The fuel consumption and exhaust emissions of oil engines did not fulfil everyone's expectations and the next development, in 1933, was an indirect injection version of the 9.12 litre engine with Ricardo-designed cylinder head. This quickly ousted the direct injection engine in the Condor. A few customers opted for Gardner engines.

By this time Crossley was established as a supplier of chassis to municipalities. Although quantities of Eagles and Alphas had been supplied to independent bus and coach operators, Crossley made no impact on the company operators and, after 1931 sold virtually no chassis to independents — a situation which changed after World War 2. Of the municipalities, Manchester was clearly the biggest customer and bought some 800 prewar chassis. The next biggest customer — Rochdale — bought only 80 and while these formed a significant part of the fleet they soon fell from popularity. Rochdale bought its last Crossley in 1935. Most other municipal customers were small and few bought more than 20 chassis in the prewar period, underlining Manchester's importance to Crossley's survival. Export business in the 1930s was negligible.

In 1934 Crossley advertised its Delta goods chassis as being suitable for bus or coach bodywork. This had a four-cylinder 3.7 litre petrol engine and could be had as a normal-control 14ft wheelbase or forward-control 12ft 6in wheelbase chassis to seat 20 passengers. Only one Delta found use as a passenger vehicle and joined the Manchester fleet in 1935.

A more significant development in 1934 was the appearance of the Mancunian. This retained the 16ft $7\frac{1}{2}$in wheelbase of the Condor but had the gearbox mounted directly behind the engine instead of amidships in the chassis. The single-decker was similarly modified but retained the Alpha name until 1938 (in theory) or 1935 (in practice). The only post-1935 single-deckers were for Manchester in 1937 and Sunderland in 1939 and all were called Mancunians. They had a later style of radiator than the Alphas.

In 1935 a short stroke version of the Crossley Ricardo indirect injection engine was installed in the Mancunian. This had a capacity of 8.37 litres and a power output of 93.5bhp, and was known as the VR6.

Meanwhile the style of the 1930s was beginning to influence a few of the larger bus operators and in 1935 Manchester revealed its designs for a streamlined bus body. This was of all-metal construction, by then standard practice at Manchester, but it featured radiused window corners and a gently curved front profile with down-swept lower edges on the front upper deck windows. An attractive livery with swoops of cream relief was also developed to produce the nearest thing to an Art Deco double-deck bus. The Manchester body style set a pattern for Crossley bodies for the following 15 years.

Crossley further modified the radiator shell of the Mancunian to match the new body — but the old style radiator remained available.

By the mid-1930s the four-speed sliding mesh gearbox had been joined by a constant mesh box but other forms of gearchanging were being tried too. As early as 1931 a preselector gearbox had been fitted to a petrol-engined Condor for Bury and in the following year a batch of preselector Condors with diesel engines went to Barrow. Northampton standardised on preselector gearboxes. A few Manchester Mancunians had synchromesh gearboxes and a Freeborn Power Converters semi-automatic unit was tried unsuccessfully by Manchester and Rochdale.

Below: This charabanc of the 1920s, surrounded by 13 young men displaying varying ideas of what constitutes sartorial elegance, was operated by Underwood of Orsett, Essex. It reputedly started life as an ambulance in World War I.
Ian Allan Library

RICKMANSWORTH
ME-6966

UXBRIDGE
MY-1959

Top left: Another early vehicle, this time with a diminutive two-door bus body, in Rickmansworth in the 1920s. The prominent radiator boss was a Crossley feature.
Ian Allan Library

Left: This Crossley became part of the London Passenger Transport Board fleet in 1933. When photographed in 1930 it was owned by Filkins & Ainsworth who operated it between Uxbridge and Harefield. A two-door 14-seat body was fitted. *Ian Allan Library*

Top: Crossley's first real bus chassis was the four-cylinder Eagle. This 1929 example belonged to Smith of Kirkcaldy and had a two-door canvas-roofed Horsfield body. Smith's business was taken over by Alexander's in 1931.
R. L. Grieves collection

Above: The fortunes of Crossley as a bus manufacturer were intertwined with those of Manchester Corporation Transport Department. This odd photo-montage produced in 1930 showed a horse bus alongside a pair of new Crossley Sixes. The one with a partly-built body carried the wording 'How your Modern Bus is constructed by Vehicle Builders at the Manchester Corporation Transport Department'. The other, with a complete MCTD 32-seat body, advised that 'The World and his Wife now travel in Comfort in the Manchester Municipal Buses built at the Manchester Corporation Transport Department'. *Ian Allan Library*

Above: The Condor was Crossley's first double-deck chassis. This example was one of the first to be built, in 1930, and had a 52-seat Brush body with a particularly striking interpretation of piano-front styling. Other notable features are the large oval rear windows on both decks and the two step platform. This bus was built as a demonstrator, registered in Glasgow, and subsequently sold to Aberdeen Corporation. *Brush*

Right: In the days before roll-on/roll-off ferries — 1930 to be precise — a new Manchester Condor is hoisted on board ship at Dover. The 48-seat lowbridge body was also a Crossley product. The occasion was a visit to France by municipal transport managers.
Ian Allan Library

Top: Leeds showed an early interest in Crossleys. This is one of five Condors purchased in 1930. The body was by Roe which was still supplying bodies to Leeds' successor, the West Yorkshire PTE, 50 years later. *Charles H. Roe*

Above: Aberdeen must have been impressed by Crossley's demonstrator because its first double-deck buses were 14 Condors purchased in 1931, to be followed by eight more in 1933. This is one of the first delivery with body by Walker of Aberdeen. They were sold in 1938/39. *W. S. Philip collection*

Above: The last of Manchester's 1930 Condors introduced a new feature to the fleet — an oil engine. The unit was a Gardner 6L2. Its installation was not designed to inspire confidence in this new means of propulsion with its prominent fuel tank and cumbersome chassis extension. Ironically, in view of the success of the diesel engine, this pioneer chassis was later converted to petrol. During its life it was twice rebodied and survived (with petrol engine) until 1946. The original body was by Crossley. *Gardner*

Right: Twelve Condors with Crossley oil engines and Strachans bodies entered service with Manchester at the end of 1931 and the beginning of 1932. This view shows clearly the imposing radiator fitted to production oil-engined Condors. *Strachans*

Above: This impressive looking Condor was one of a batch which joined the Barrow fleet in 1932. It had a Crossley oil engine and a preselector gearbox. The 48-seat body was by Northern Counties. *Gavin Booth collection*

Centre left: Portsmouth's 1932 Condors were long-lived. This is a postwar view of one of 20 which were purchased with English Electric bodywork. *V. C. Jones*

Bottom left: This Burnley Corporation Tramways & Omnibuses' Condor also dates from 1932 but has very conservative 48-seat bodywork by Brush. It was one of a pair which were the last buses to be purchased by Burnley before the formation of the Burnley, Colne and Nelson Joint Transport Committee in April 1933. Both buses were short-lived. The chassis, which had oil engines and preselector gearboxes, were sold for spares to Rochdale Corporation; the bodies were mounted on new AEC Regent chassis in 1936. *Brush*

Right: The last of a batch of 30 Condors delivered to Manchester in 1932 had a prototype all-metal body by Metro-Cammell featuring five-bay construction. Even by 1949, when this photograph was taken, the body looked passably modern. *R. Marshall*

Below: The Mancunian had the same radiator shell as the Condor which it replaced but had a close-coupled engine and gearbox and a left hand gear lever. This 1934 example in the Manchester fleet had a Metro-Cammell body and was one of the first batch of production Mancunians. Most early Mancunians purchased by Manchester survived until 1949/50, although not necessarily with their original bodywork. *G. H. F. Atkins*

Left: In 1934 this normal-control Alpha was exported to South Africa where it operated for Durban Corporation. It had a Crossley 9.12-litre oil engine which returned a fuel consumption of 11mpg. No more Crossleys found buyers in South Africa. *Ian Allan Library*

Below: Another oddity was the unique three-axle Mancunian. This 63-seater must have seemed enormous when it took to the road in 1934. It had a Crossley body which was completed by Manchester Corporation for which it ran — infrequently — until 1946 when it was sold for scrap. *R. Marshall collection*

Above: Northampton bought 25 Crossley double-deckers in the 1930s. This is a 1934 Condor, among the last of the type to be built, with 54-seat Crossley body. It is seen during the war with masked headlamps and white painted wings.
T. W. Moore collection

Below: Two Mancunians with Northern Counties bodies and Gardner 6LW engines joined the Cardiff fleet in 1935 and ran until 1949. *T. W. Moore collection*

Below: Manchester bought 20 Alphas in 1934 and these had Crossley bodies on Metro-Cammell frames. They were 32-seaters of rear-entrance layout. The Alpha had a shorter radiator shell than the Mancunian double-decker.
R. Marshall collection

Bottom: Oddest of all prewar Crossley single-deckers was the only Delta to be used as a psv. This 20-seat coach had a Crossley four-cylinder petrol engine and a Crossley body. It was purchased by Manchester Corporation in 1935 for use on a service to the airport.
Greater Manchester Transport Museum Society

Above: The Manchester streamlines epitomise the 1930s interest in things modern. The body has subtle curves; the paint scheme features bold sweeps of cream relief. Even when it was standing still the Manchester streamline design suggested movement. The first streamlines appeared in 1936 — three years before London Transport's RT design. By comparison with the RT, the Manchester design was ephemeral. But is was also a much more adventurous, more eye-catching exercise. Could any citizen of Manchester have failed to notice the arrival of a new breed of bus? This 1937 example was exhibited at that year's Commercial Motor Show and had an English Electric/Crossley body. Crossley also provided a new wide radiator shell to blend with the body lines. This 52-seater weighed just under 7 tons unladen. *Ian Allan Library*

Right: Meanwhile, Sunderland Corporation's contribution to modern bus design came in the shape of a pair of Mancunians with 48-seat fully-fronted English Electric bodies. The overall appearance was not unlike that of a tramcar. This bus was new in 1937. *Tyne & Wear PTE*

Below: An interesting addition to the Ashton-under-Lyne fleet in 1937 was this Alpha. It was one of a pair built in 1933. The other went to Australia and this one was destined for New Zealand — a frustrated export order, to coin a phrase. The 32-seat body was also by Crossley. *Ian Allan Library*

Bottom: In 1937 Manchester received 20 single-deck Mancunians with streamlined Metro-Cammell/Crossley bodies, again of 32-seat rear-entrance layout. These had the same wide radiators as used on the streamlined double deckers. *R. Marshall collection*

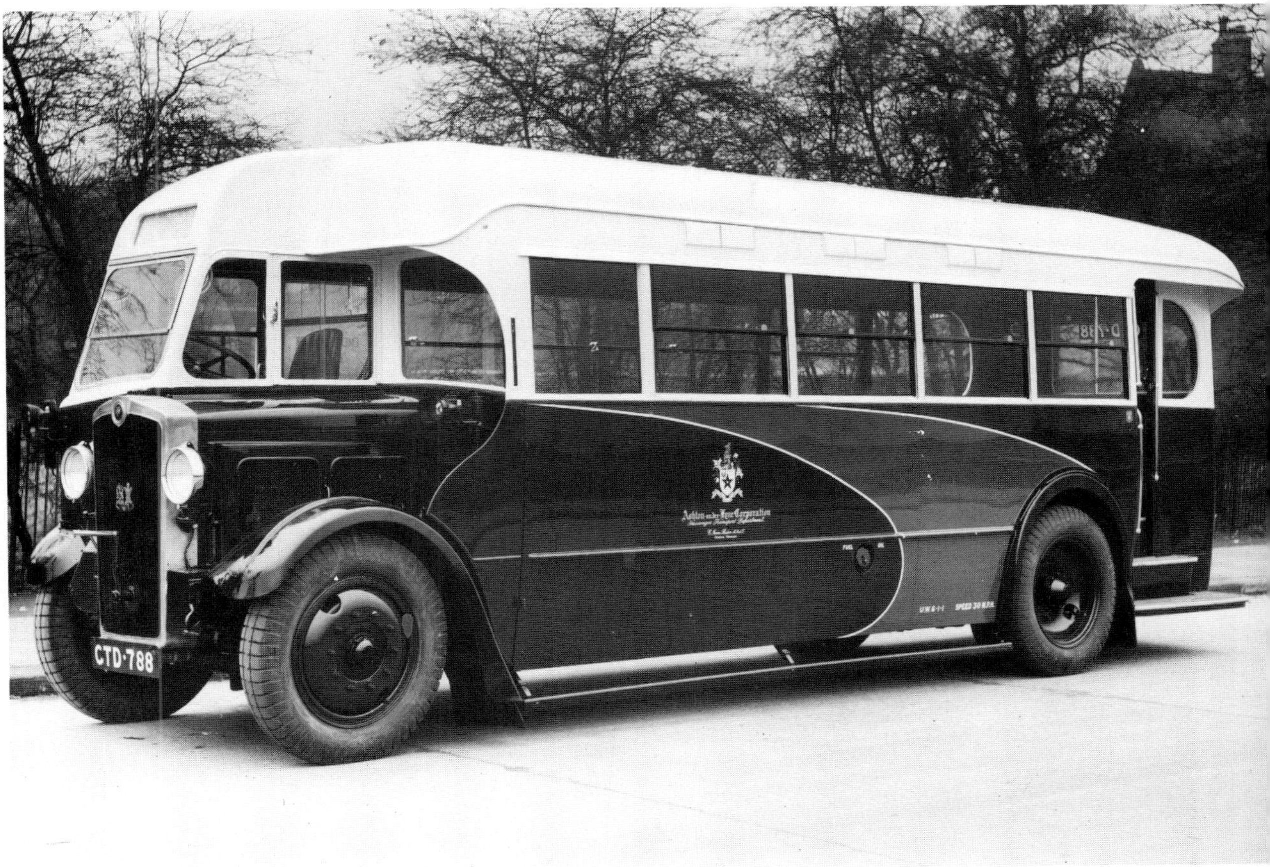

Above: A 1938 Mancunian with Metro-Cammell/Crossley 54-seat body in Manchester Piccadilly, overlooked by the massive art deco Rylands department store. *R. Marshall*

Below: From modernity to antiquity. Between 1934 and 1940 Maidstone Corporation bought on average two Crossley oil-engined double-deckers each year. The 1938 delivery is shown here — two Mancunians with Gardner 5LW power units and rather dated six-bay Crossley bodywork which with its ornate lining out, louvred glass vents, and vintage sidelamps seems years behind contemporary Manchester practice. These buses were replaced by Leyland Titan PD2s in 1956. *Ian Allan Library*

Top: The last Mancunian single-deckers were a pair supplied in 1939 to Sunderland Corporation and bodied locally by Blagg. *Tyne & Wear PTE*

Above: Two Mancunians joined the Stockport fleet in 1941 and were the last of the type to be built. Both had Metro-Cammell/Crossley streamlined bodywork which looks a bit unhappy in standard Stockport livery, devoid of the exuberant sweeps of relief colour used in neighbouring Manchester. This is a 1957 view. Both buses were sold in 1958. *A. Moyes*

Trolleybuses

Despite the opposition of its transport committee, Manchester Corporation decided in 1935 to replace tramcars with trolleybuses. And so it came to pass that in 1936 Crossley introduced its trolleybus range. First came the TDD6 (**T**rolleybus **D**ouble **D**eck **6** wheel), a three-axle design of 18ft 7in wheelbase, and then the two-axle TDD4 which had a 16ft wheelbase — 7½in shorter than the Mancunian from which it was derived. Metrovick electrical equipment was standard and a total of 17 TDD6 and 97 TDD4 was built before the war brought production to a halt. Most of these joined the Manchester fleet.

Production recommenced after the war. The four-wheeler was now the TDD42 and the six-wheeler the TDD64. But customers were few: Manchester (TDD42/1 and TDD64/1), Ashton (TDD42/2) and Cleethorpes (TDD42/3). The four-wheeler received the model name Empire while the six-wheeler was called the Dominion. The wheelbases were the same as on prewar models.

For export markets the Transit model trolleybus was advertised. This was designed for 8ft wide, 33ft 7in long bodywork and had a 17ft wheelbase with an amidships mounted motor and a set back front axle which allowed a front entrance. Fourteen vehicles of this layout went to New Zealand.

Below: The first Crossley trolleybus was a three-axle TDD6 with a Crossley built body on Metro-Cammell frames. It was registered by Crossley in 1936 and then operated on hire to Ashton-under-Lyne by which it was purchased in 1938.
NW Museum of Science & Industry

Top left: The 1937 prototype TDD4 was a much more modern looking vehicle. It too had a Metro-Cammell/Crossley body but the restrained livery and radiused window corners give a well-balanced appearance which would not have looked out of place 10 years later. The only odd feature is the downward slope towards the rear of the canopy above the platform. *NW Museum of Science & Industry*

Centre left: Manchester's first trolleybuses were ordered at the beginning of 1937 and the system was inaugurated on 1 March 1938. Among the first vehicles were 28 TDD4 with Metro-Cammell/Crossley streamlined bodies. A further 40 were delivered in the early years of the war. There were also 12 TDD6 three-axle vehicles. All had Metropolitan Vickers motors. *W. J. Haynes*

Below: Two TDD6 were delivered to Belfast in 1938 to take part in comparative trials with six other manufacturers' vehicles. This one was shipped from Liverpool complete with 68-seat Crossley body. Its partner was bodied in Belfast by Harkness. Belfast eventually placed bulk orders with AEC — but the two Crossleys could not have been too bad: they survived until 1958. *Ian Allan Library*

Right: The only large batch of trolleybuses for a customer other than Manchester or Ashton went to Hull in 1938. Twenty of these TDD4 with austere-looking Craven bodywork were purchased. The streamlined livery was less exciting, but longer lasting, than that used by Manchester. The use of dark lettering on a light background for the destination screens is unusual.
Ian Allan Library

Below: Ashton purchased eight Crossley TDD4 in 1940, all with Metro-Cammell/ Crossley bodywork. The red, white and blue Ashton livery was beautifully executed but harked back to an earlier era; the white lining on the wings is a gentle reminder that there is a war on.
Ian Allan Library

Top left: A 1950 Empire TDD42/2 in the Ashton fleet makes an interesting comparison with its prewar counterpart in the previous picture. The Crossley body still shows its streamlined ancestry. But by 1961, when this photograph was taken, complex liveries had vanished. Ashton had five trolleybuses of this type. *R. L. Wilson*

Centre left: The last Crossleys to enter service in Manchester were 16 Dominion TDD64/1 three-axle trolleybuses with 66-seat Crossley bodywork. They were new in 1951 and were the only postwar three-axle trolleybuses built by Crossley. The extra bay has shallow windows and unbalances the vehicle's lines. All were withdrawn in 1963. *R. Marshall*

Below: Crossley's last trolleybuses were a pair supplied to Cleethorpes Corporation in 1951. These had Roe bodywork and ended their days in Walsall where they carried the label 'trolleybus' on the front panel lest anyone be in doubt what this silent flat-fronted vehicle might be. This TDD42/3 is seen on training duties in 1970. *T. W. Moore*

Postwar years

The Gorton works were badly damaged in December 1940 and wartime production was concentrated on military vehicles. But one interesting bus was still to appear before postwar production got under way — the prototype DD42/1. This had a new Crossley 8.6 litre oil engine, type HOE7, and a Brockhouse Turbo Transmitter — which featured a torque convertor — instead of a conventional gearbox. It had a new narrower radiator with parallel sides and a small Maltese cross motif. Postwar production models had a similar radiator but it was mounted lower.

All postwar Crossley motorbuses had HOE7 engines; the last buses to have the optional Gardner power unit were two 5LW-engined Mancunians for Maidstone in 1938. The basic models were the DD42 and SD42, respectively **D**ouble **D**eck and **S**ingle **D**eck chassis with **4** wheels, **2** of which were driven.

Introduced in 1946, the DD42 had a 16ft 7½in wheelbase — the same as the prewar Mancunian — and a choice of gearboxes: constant mesh or Brockhouse Turbo Transmitter. A synchromesh gearbox was soon added to the range. Model variants were identified by suffix numbers and the full postwar range comprised:

DD42/3	7ft 6in wide
DD42/4	8ft wide
DD42/5	revised 7ft 6in wide
DD42/6	Birmingham model
DD42/7	modified engine, 7ft 6in wide
DD42/8	modified engine, 8ft wide
DD42/8A	improved suspension

A T suffix was added to models fitted with the torque convertor gearbox.

In the early postwar years when demand for new double-deck buses outstripped supply, Crossley found a wider range of municipal customers and a few independents too. Independent coach operators bought large numbers of Crossley single-deckers — almost 650 out of some 750 home market SD42 chassis went to independents.

Production of the SD42 commenced in 1947 and the range for British operators was:

SD42/3	7ft 6in wide
SD42/5	8ft wide
SD42/6	7ft 6in wide
SD42/7	7ft 6in wide, modified engine, optional five-speed gearbox
SD42/8	8ft wide, modified engine

All of these had a 17ft 7in wheelbase but in 1950 two 19ft 3in wheelbase models were introduced to accommodate 30ft long bodywork. These were:

SD42/9	7ft 6in wide
SD42/9A	8ft wide

Both SD42/9 variants had a five-speed gearbox as standard.

The postwar range initially had a radiator featuring the Maltese cross motif but in 1948 the Crossley name was substituted for the motif. Some later vehicles had chromed radiator shells, sometimes with a vertical central strip on SD42 chassis. However, radiators were interchangeable and in later life early postwar chassis could be seen with later style radiators and vice versa. The low-mounted radiator was one of Crossley's distinctive features.

Generally, Crossley did little export business — but its one big order was one of the most surprising chapters in the annals of Britain's overseas bus business. This was an order for a record total of 1,175 buses for the Netherlands Railways — a record which is still unbroken and looks likely to remain so.

The Netherlands Railways required a mixture of chassis. The oddest were 250 normal-control tractor units which were virtually standard chassis with the centre section removed and the driving position relocated. Wide ratio gearboxes were fitted and these models were classified type PT42/1, PT indicating **P**assenger **T**ractor. There were also 500 SD42/1 and 425 SD42/2 — these had wheelbases of, respectively, 20ft 3½in and 18ft 0½in. Both types had five-speed gearboxes.

The HOE7 engine was generally rated to produce 100bhp but the version used in the home market SD42/9 (and some SD42/7) was rated at 112bhp. In the SD42/1 for Netherlands Railways a supercharged version, the HOE9, was used and could produce up to 150bhp.

Crossley was still active in the bodybuilding business after the war and the postwar double-deck body owed much to the prewar Manchester streamline design. A few customers even specified streamlined liveries. The most obvious change to the body was the stepped window line. The two rearmost side windows on each deck were shallower than the main side windows to accommodate supports for the rear platform. Not all operators wanted swept down corners on the front windows and later bodies also did away with the step in the waistline. Attractive four-bay bodywork was built for Liverpool and Rotherham;

the standard Crossley body had five bays.

Crossley had moved to Errwood Park, Stockport, in 1946, which may have influenced Stockport Corporation's purchasing policy in the late 1940s. In 1948 Crossley Motors was taken over by AEC which, in the same year, also purchased the Maudslay business. The controlling group was titled Associated Commercial Vehicles Ltd and in 1949 it was further expanded by the acquisition of the coachbuilding businesses of Park Royal and Charles H. Roe.

At the start of the 1950s the postwar boom in the bus and coach business came to an end, and with it ACV's requirement for chassis from Crossley. In 1950 Crossley's range was augmented by the Mark IV — but this was none other than the AEC-produced Regal IV. In 1951 all of AEC's home market models were being listed as Crossleys. The 9621E Regal III for instance became the Crossley C9621E. Very few AECs were actually built with Crossley badges but this ploy did give the ACV group an extra stand at the Earls Court Commercial Motor Show.

The last Crossley DD42 entered service in 1952, the last SD42 in 1953. That was not quite the end of the story. Much of the development work on the ACV group's Bridgemaster was carried out at Stockport and it was first shown to the public as a Crossley Bridgemaster. But production was always planned to be in the hands of AEC and Park Royal. Crossley also assembled BUT trolleybus chassis on behalf of ACV and continued to build double-deck bus bodies — until 1957 when the axe finally fell and Crossley Motors Ltd was closed.

Above: The prototype of the postwar DD42 series entered service with Manchester Corporation in 1944. It was type DD42/1 and had a short radiator — which set the style for postwar models — but retained the traditional high mounting position. The body was a 1939 Metro-Cammell/Crossley removed from a Mancunian. An 8.6 litre HOE7 engine and Brockhouse Turbo-Transmitter were fitted. By the time this photograph was taken in 1957 the bus was running with a Leyland engine and gearbox. It was sold for scrap in 1963. *R. Marshall*

Left: Bolton's first new buses since 1943 arrived in 1946 — the start of a delivery of 75 Crossley DD42/3s. All were delivered by 1947 and allowed the closure of the municipal tramway system in March of that year. Eight had Crossley bodies; the remaining 67 had utilitarian-looking Craven bodywork as shown here. This order made Bolton Crossley's third-biggest postwar British customer after Manchester and Birmingham. Four single-deck Crossleys were added to the Bolton fleet in 1949, but most of Bolton's postwar business went to Leyland. The 1946 Crossleys were withdrawn between 1959 and 1962. *A. Moyes*

Above: Ten Crossleys delivered in 1946 temporarily broke Northampton's loyalty to Daimler. These were Roe-bodied DD42/3s and were the first peacetime postwar deliveries to Northampton. Two are seen in the town centre in 1959. *T. W. Moore*

Centre right: A handful of early postwar double-deck chassis received single-deck bodywork. This DD42/3 of Reliance, Great Gonerby, was new in 1946 with 35-seat Willowbrook bodywork. *G. R. Mills*

Bottom right: In 1946 three DD42/3s were fitted with fully-fronted Strachans coach bodies. This one was delivered to Partridge of Layham, whose depot it is seen leaving in 1961. The full front was a fairly unusual feature in 1946. *G. R. Mills*

Above: Manchester's first postwar Crossleys arrived in 1946. These were DD42/3s with Crossley's own standard postwar body which in some respects was a restrained version of the prewar Manchester streamline. This bus was the only one to be delivered with platform doors. Some of these vehicles were later fitted with Leyland 8.6 litre engines and the few which had Turbo-Transmitters later received Leyland gearboxes. *Ian Allan Library*

Below: In 1947 Cardiff Corporation purchased two DD42/3s from the Almondsbury Engineering Company. These had 56-seat bodywork by Scottish Commercial, Crossley's Glasgow agent. The front upper deck window line shows Crossley influence. These two buses, along with a similar vehicle diverted from Almondsbury before delivery in 1948, were withdrawn in 1961. *Don Morris*

Above: Between 1946 and 1951 a total of 65 Crossley double-deckers joined the Stockport fleet: during this period Crossley's bus manufacturing was carried on in Stockport. This 1947 DD42/3 is seen passing Battersby's hat factory at Offerton in 1965. The distinctive lines of the standard Crossley body are clearly seen; the swept down upper deck front windows; the deep driver's windscreen; and the shallow rear side windows necessitated by the method Crossley used for supporting the rear platform. *A. Moyes*

Centre right: Chesterfield Corporation bought 30 double-deck Crossleys including this 1947 DD42/5. Lowbridge Crossley bodywork was supplied to only five DD42 customers. *A. Moyes*

Bottom right: A trio of all-Crossley DD42/3s ready for delivery to South Shields Corporation in 1947. The streamlined livery, which by then had been abandoned by Manchester, is a splendid anachronism. The original postwar radiator with the Crossley emblem can be clearly seen.
NW Museum of Science & Industry

Left: In 1948 Eastbourne Corporation bought AECs, Leylands and Crossleys. The latter were eight DD42/5s with East Lancs bodywork having the unusually low seating capacity of 50. These were Eastbourne's only Crossleys and were the only DD42s to be bodied by East Lancs. They were withdrawn in 1962/3.
R. L. Wilson

Below: Some surprising operators specified streamlined paint schemes. This 1947 DD42 was for a Scottish independent, Duncan of Law in Lanarkshire. Although the paint scheme follows the South Shields pattern the body is different. It lacks the curved lower edges on the front upper deck windows while the inclusion of a gutter above the windows hides the radiused top corners. A different style of top-sliding ventilator is used, too.
A. J. Douglas collection

Above: Crossley supplied 10 chassis to Uruguay. This long-wheelbase SD42/1 had a 37-seat body built in Montevideo. The massive front bumper hints at local driving standards! *Ian Allan Library*

Centre right: The last Crossley motorbuses for Manchester Corporation were 8ft wide DD42/8 models which entered service in 1948/49. This 1948 example is seen in 1966 by which time a very simple livery is in use: all-over red relieved by a single cream band. The curved bottom edges of the front windows hark back to the daring streamline design of 30 years earlier. The last DD42/8 was withdrawn in 1968, ending 40 years of Crossley operation by Manchester Corporation. *G. R. Mills*

Bottom right: Crossley centre-entrance 42-seat bodywork was fitted to this SD42 for the Netherlands Railways. It was one of 150 similar vehicles and was new in 1948. *Ian Allan Library*

Above: A pair of Crossley PT42/1s for the Netherlands Railways. These had DAF semi-trailers and bodywork by a consortium of Verheul, Fokker and Aviolanda. They fulfilled a need for high capacity buses and were delivered in 1946/47. A total of 250 were built and they had 52-seat (plus 28 standee) bodywork. Two spare wheels were carried behind the tractor cab. They were 14 metres (46ft) long. *courtesy J. F. J. Kuipers*

Below: Scottish Commercial ordered six DD42s with lowbridge Roe bodywork. These were sold to Wemyss of Ardersier, Smith of Barrhead, A1 Service of Ardrossan, and Baxter of Airdrie, who bought three. One of the Baxter buses is seen in Coatbridge. *Stewart J. Brown collection*

Right: One of 14 Roe-bodied SD42s in the Oldham fleet is seen at Mossley in the summer of 1963. New in 1948, it was sold in 1966. *A. Moyes*

Below: Gash of Newark, best known as a Daimler operator, purchased this Yeates-bodied SD42 in 1948. The peaked destination boxes were a Yeates hallmark. The windscreen takes full advantage of the low Crossley radiator which on this vehicle has the later type of badge with the Crossley name in place of the Maltese cross emblem. *G. R. Mills*

Top left: The only postwar Crossley to be bodied by Massey joined the Colchester fleet in 1948. Built as a DD42/3T it had its torque convertor removed before entering passenger service. It was withdrawn in 1968. *G. R. Mills*

Centre left: In the late 1940s Crossleys were popular with independent coach operators. This SD42 with Duple 35-seat coach body was new to Jackson of Castle Bromwich but was owned by Smith of Axford when photographed in 1958. *T. W. W. Knowles*

Below: Crossley's standard single-deck body bore a strong family resemblance to the double-deck product as can be seen on this 1949 SD42/7 of Chesterfield Corporation. The body had 32 seats and a rear entrance. It is seen outside the Town Hall in 1961. *A. Moyes*

Above: The chromed radiator and polished wheel rings give this 1949 SD42 coach a fresh appearance. It was new to Auty of Bury — a regular Crossley customer — but was photographed running for Payne of Bedworth. The 33-seat bodywork was by County of Leigh, one of the numerous small bodybuilders which flourished briefly in the postwar coaching boom. *Don Morris*

Centre right: Few single-deckers received what were commonly known as 'new look' fronts. The attractive Birmingham style bonnet and grille are fitted to this SD42 of Harper of Heath Hayes. This bus was new to Silcox of Pembroke Dock who also built the body. *A. J. Douglas*

Bottom right: Dunkerley of Royton was the proud owner of this SD42 with stepped-waist body by Challenger. The styling is striking, but hardly modern by the standards of 1949. The emblem on the side reads 'Swift & Sure' and features a Tiger's head which might have been more at home on a contemporary Leyland model! *NW Museum of Science & Industry*

Top: Only one batch of Crossleys was bought by an operator in the British Electric Traction group of companies. Western Welsh operated 37 of these 32-seat Willowbrook-bodied SD42s. New in 1949, this one is seen in Bridgend in 1960. *A. Moyes*

Above: Handsome Burlingham bodywork was fitted to this SD42 which had the distinction of being operated by Crosville before joining the fleet of Williams of Lythfaen on the Lleyn Peninsula. It was new in 1949 to yet another Welsh operator — Ellis of Llanllechid. *R. L. Wilson*

Top: Mainwairing Brothers of Bignall End owned three Crossley double-deckers when they sold out to Potteries Motor Traction in June 1951. This DD42/7 with lowbridge Crossley body was new in 1949 and ran for PMT until 1960. It sports a PMT radiator badge in place of its original Crossley one. *A. D. Broughall*

Above: A 1950 all-Crossley DD42/8 with chromed radiator shell in the fleet of Oldham Corporation. Oldham ran 14 Crossley 'deckers. *A. D. Broughall*

Above and below: Birmingham was an important postwar customer with 270 double-deckers being purchased in 1949/50, all with Crossley bodywork to Birmingham design. Both vehicles illustrated here were new in 1950 and are DD42/7s — but the new look front coupled to some tidying up of bodywork details creates an impression of a more modern vehicle. The last 100 of Birmingham's Crossleys had new look fronts; the others had exposed radiators.
T. W. Moore

Above: Reading Corporation's only Crossleys were 12 DD42/8 delivered in 1950. All had 52-seat lowbridge Crossley bodywork without the stepped window line which had previously been a characteristic Crossley feature. They also had platform doors, an item fitted to all subsequent Reading buses but still quite remarkable in 1950. They were long-lived, being sold in 1967/68.
ACV Sales

Centre right: Although real Crossleys were still being built and were still entering service, Associated Commercial Vehicles indulged in some blatant badge engineering at the 1950 Commercial Motor Show. Did anyone really believe that this exhibit on Crossley's stand was anything other than an AEC Regent III?
Ian Allan Library

Bottom right: Two Strachans-bodied DD42s entered service with Gibson Brothers of Barlestone in 1950.
Strachans

Left: Coventry Corporation's sole Crossley was a 1951 DD42/7T. Its Brockhouse Turbo-Transmitter was soon replaced by an AEC crash gearbox and the 7.7 litre AEC engine which went with it. It later received a Daimler preselector gearbox. Metro-Cammell 58-seat bodywork was fitted and Coventry's dark maroon and cream livery was applied in a reversed style. This city centre photograph was taken in 1960. *T. W. Moore*

Below: Molins Machinery of Saunderton bought three all-Crossley SD42s in 1951. This one, seen after being purchased by Williams of Wrexham, has the chromed radiator with central dividing strip which was a feature of some of the later chassis. It ran for Williams until 1967. *A. D. Broughall*

Top right: In 1951/52 Colchester Corporation purchased four DD42/7s. Three of them are seen here in 1967, demonstrating how different livery applications alter the appearance of the standard Crossley body. The last vestiges of streamlining have now gone, apart from the drooping cab window line. All were sold in 1968. *G. R. Mills*

Centre right: Two long-wheelbase SD42/9 coaches were purchased by the Royal Navy at Portsmouth in 1952 and had Strachans bodywork. This one is seen 10 years later at the Kursaal coach park in Southend, operating for Brown Brothers. *G. R. Mills*

Below: Derby bought five DD42/8A with 8ft wide Brush bodywork in 1952. This 1964 view shows one in the brighter livery then used by Derby. When new, the area between decks was painted dark green. *T. W. Moore*

Top: Darwen fleet numbers never got higher then 44. The first 44 was this 1952 DD42/7, one of 10 bought between 1949 and 1952. It is seen loading in the Circus in 1962.
A. Moyes

Above: Rotherham only started buying Crossleys in 1949, and in 1952 received the last to be built. These had attractive four-bay Crossley bodywork reminiscent of a design built for Liverpool a few years earlier. *A. Moyes*

Above: Three SD42/9A chassis with Mann Egerton half-deck coach bodywork were purchased by Creamline of Bordon in 1952. They seated 48 passengers, though storing 48 suitcases must have presented problems. They could hardly be described as attractive vehicles. *T. W. Moore collection*

Below: The badge says Crossley — but the AEC wings give the game away. This Crossley Regal Mark IV with Whitson 41-seat Grand Prix Luxury Coach bodywork was one of a number of spurious Crossley models. The Crossley name effectively gave AEC another stand at Commercial Motor Shows — this one was in 1952. *Gavin Booth collection*

Above and left: There was more justification in applying the Crossley name to the Bridgemaster. Although it was an AEC design, much of the development work was done at Crossley and the first vehicle had a Crossley body and a Crossley badge on its radiator. The artist's impression makes it look sleeker than it really was, and revives the Maltese cross on the radiator. The real thing, which was exhibited at the 1956 Commercial Motor Show before entering service with Walsall Corporation, is quite obviously a thinly-disguised AEC. *ACV Sales, T. W. Moore*

Above: End of the road. Warwickshire, August 1964.
T. W. Moore